DIGITAL AND INFORMATION LITERACY ™

FREEDOM OF SPEECH OR DEFAMATION? EXPRESSING YOURSELF ON THE WEB

JASON PORTERFIELD

rosen publishing's
rosen central®

New York

Published in 2013 by The Rosen Publishing Group, Inc.
29 East 21st Street, New York, NY 10010

Copyright © 2013 by The Rosen Publishing Group, Inc.

First Edition

Library of Congress Cataloging-in-Publication Data

Porterfield, Jason.
Freedom of speech or defamation?: expressing yourself on the Web/Jason Porterfield.
— 1st ed.
        p. cm.—(Digital and information literacy)
Includes bibliographical references and index.
ISBN 978-1-4488-8356-1 (library binding)—
ISBN 978-1-4488-8370-7 (pbk)—
ISBN 978-1-4488-8371-4 (6-pack)
1. Freedom of speech—United States. 2. Libel and slander—United States. I. Title.
JC599.U5P57 2013
323.44'30973—dc23

                                                  2012024920

Manufactured in the United States of America

CPSIA Compliance Information: Batch #W13YA: For further information, contact Rosen Publishing, New York, New York, at 1-800-237-9932.

CONTENTS

INTRODUCTION

Freedom of speech is one of the most basic liberties enjoyed by Americans. When Congress drafted the Bill of Rights in 1787, its members considered freedom of speech to be so important that they made it part of the First Amendment. This amendment states: "Congress shall make no law respecting an establishment of religion, or prohibiting the free exercise thereof; or abridging the freedom of speech, or of the press; or the right of the people peaceably to assemble, and to petition the Government for a redress of grievances." The nation's founders believed that in order for a democracy to work, people must be able to express themselves without fear of punishment. The freedom of speech that they included in the Bill of Rights gives people the right to publicly speak their minds. There are very few types of speech that are not protected by the First Amendment.

Defamation is one of those types of unprotected speech. Defamation is the publication of a statement of an alleged fact that is untrue and is harmful to the reputation of another person. There are two types of defamation: libel and slander. Slander is usually defined as an untrue statement about a person that is spoken out loud, such as a rumor being spread. Libel is an untrue statement that can be seen, usually in writing.

Libel and slander can both be harmful to a person's reputation. Slander might have a more immediate impact on your reputation if it spreads quickly,

The Internet brings a vast amount of information right to a computer user's fingertips. Sorting through this data in order to figure out what is accurate can be a daunting task.

but it then fades away, while libelous statements may stay in print for some time. Defamation that takes place online is almost always libel, though the defamatory comments posted on message boards or social media sites might spread even faster than a rumor spoken on the street.

The consequences of defamation can be painful. The defamed person may see his or her relationships and business dealings suffer as the rumor spreads. Even if the rumor is proven to be false, there may still be some people who refuse to believe the truth. This can be particularly true for rumors spread online, which may spread to many sites and be very difficult to escape. Defamed people sometimes have their entire lives uprooted.

There can also be legal consequences for the defamer. If the defamed person can prove who made the defamatory comments, that person can be sued for damages. In some states, criminal charges can be brought against a person who defames another.

There are also cases in which people are falsely or incorrectly accused of defamation. Defamation laws establish several broad defenses against such charges. The rapid exchange of information on the Internet makes it easier for people to disseminate falsehoods, even if they don't know that they are spreading lies. The best way to avoid these situations is to stay civil online and be careful about what you post.

Chapter 1

Choosing Sources

In North America, the Internet is a place where virtually anyone can express an opinion about anything. There are message boards and discussion groups for many different interests, such as sports, hobbies, politics, video games, and books. People post reviews of restaurants, car repair tips, vacation stories, and information about pet care. Some of the information found online is accurate and helpful. Some is not. Rumors and misinformation are also common online.

Online social media and networking tools such as Twitter, Tumbler, and Facebook make it quick and easy to communicate news to a large number of people. Unfortunately, these tools also make it easier for rumors and misinformation to spread quickly.

The Internet offers a great deal of freedom to express yourself. You can present yourself in a way that is totally different from how you may act in school or around your friends and family. Your posts can let people you know see another side of yourself or help you reach out to people you've never met. The Internet is in many ways a wide-open place where people can express themselves freely and share their knowledge and experiences. Unfortunately, not all of the information that is found online is true or trustworthy.

Social networking Web sites such as Facebook make it easy for people to connect with their friends, acquaintances, and "followers." Such sites help people share information, messages, and opinions with others instantaneously.

Freedom of Speech Online

Freedom of speech is one of the most celebrated aspects of the Internet. Many Internet users have opposed restrictions on what is said and how opinions are expressed online. They appreciate being able to share their ideas with others across long distances without worrying about being silenced.

However, not everyone who uses the Internet behaves in a respectful manner. Some people go out of their way to harass others. They may target people they know or total strangers. They may have grudges against their targets, or they may pick them at random. This behavior is often considered cyberbullying or cyberstalking. Today, many schools have rules against cyberstalking and cyberbullying. Likewise, most states have laws against cyberstalking, and many have passed cyberbullying laws in recent years.

Harassing people on message boards, in forums, or in chat rooms is often called "trolling" because the harasser is behaving like a mean-spirited troll. Many message board and chat room visitors accept trolls as a hazard of being online. They don't like the activity, but there isn't much they can do

✉ **New message from Here2BugU**　⊗

SUBJECT:　(no subject)

MESSAGE:　if you don't reply to this, i'm gonna tell everyone at school that ur a loser! CHICKEN!!!

WHAT DO YOU DO?

Reply

Ignore

Online harassment can take many forms, from rude "trolling" behavior by strangers visiting message boards to threatening messages or false information posted by bullies at school.

about it except inform the board's moderators or navigate away from the site and hope the troll goes away. Message boards and forums often have policies against trolling behavior, and users who violate those rules may find themselves banned from the site.

Other people may post information online that they know is false in an effort to mislead their readers. Their work may be presented to look like a reputable source. The question that a Web surfer has to ask is whether a site is being misleading for humorous purposes, whether the misinformation is unintentional, or whether it is deliberately misleading.

Online defamation is common. People use their Web sites, message boards, and other platforms to spread rumors and lies about others. Anyone can be a target, from celebrities and politicians to classmates and friends. Sometimes this is done as a joke, but more often it is meant to hurt the person in some way. Reputations can be damaged by lies posted online.

Evaluating Sources

If you're putting together a Web site that is meant to present factual information, be sure that you find good sources for your material. Sources can sometimes be hard to judge. Official Web sites are often good places to start looking. Web sites for newspapers, magazines, and journals often have unbiased and factual information. Other news media outlets, such as television networks, radio stations, and online news outlets, can also be good sources.

One good way to find factual sources is to look at the bibliographies and footnotes found in books, magazines, journals, and even some Web sites. Do the sources that are cited by your source seem reliable and trustworthy? News media outlets usually attribute information to sources within the text, so check to see whose words are quoted or referred to in a story.

When you're writing about a particular person, group, or even a company, it is important to use the best sources you can find. Telling people where you found the information is a good way to show that you have done your research. Quotes from articles or other posts, snippets of video and

The Library of Congress   >> Switch to Library of Congress Authorities

LIBRARY OF CONGRESS ONLINE CATALOG

About Displaying and Searching Using Non-Roman Characters
Frequently Asked Questions - Help Contents - Requesting Materials Online

QUICK SEARCH: [   ]   Keyword (All) ▼   (Search)

Basic Search

Using a fill-in box, search by:

- Title or Author/Creator
- Subject
- Call number
- LCCN, ISSN, or ISBN
- Keywords

Note: Search limits are available only for title and keyword searches.

Guided Search

Using a series of forms and menus:

- Construct keyword searches
- Restrict all or part of the search to a particular index
- Combine search words or phrases with Boolean operators

Note: Search limits are available for all searches.

Other Online Catalogs:

Prints and Photographs Online Catalog (PPOC)

Sound Online Inventory & Catalog (SONIC) | about

E-Resources Online Catalog

Handbook of Latin American Studies (HLAS Web)

Alternative Interface to the LC Online Catalog (Z39.50)

Copyright Registrations/Docs

Other Libraries' Catalogs

Information about the images: Two pendentive paintings by Edward J. Holslag are displayed from the Librarian's Room (Librarian's Ceremonial Office) located in the Thomas Jefferson Building of the Library of Congress. On the left, "Efficiunt clarum studio" (Study, the watchword of fame); on the right, "Dulce ante omnia musae" (The Muses, above all things, delightful).

The Library of Congress
May 15, 2012

Contact Us

Sometimes it can be hard to figure out whether information found online can be trusted. Information posted by established organizations and government entities such as the Library of Congress (http://catalog.loc.gov) is almost always reliable.

audio, and links to Web sites that served as sources can all be added to a post to provide supporting information for your writing.

Avoid using information that appears untrustworthy, nonobjective, or biased; that is not attributed to a source; or that takes away from the rest of your writing. Presenting a rumor as a fact can have damaging consequences if the rumor hurts another person. The same is true of insults. Both can be considered defamation. Information from sources that are obviously biased against a group or individual should also be avoided unless it is presented in a balanced fashion alongside information arguing the opposite point.

Be careful when using message boards as sources for information. The Internet allows people to hide their true identities or even present themselves as someone else. People pose as celebrities, professionals, and experts in order to gain an audience that they may not otherwise attract. However, message boards can help point toward factual information. Compare information on a message board to facts found in trusted sources. Does the message board information line up with the confirmed facts? Do a little research to see if information on message boards can be confirmed in other places. If so, it may be better to cite those other, better trusted, clearly reputable sources.

One good way to verify information found online is to see if it matches information found in other sources, such as magazine articles and books.

Protected Opinions

Information that is presented as opinion is usually protected from allegations of defamation. Freedom of speech means being able to express your views in public without fear of being punished. Negative reviews of an artistic effort or performance or critical interpretations of current events are included in these protections.

Freedom of speech is a great responsibility. While the Bill of Rights guarantees the right to speak one's mind, there are also laws in place to protect people against defamation. While opinions are protected, individuals may have grounds for legal action if they become the target of name-calling and personal attacks.

File   Edit   View   Favorites   Tools   Help

PRIVILEGE AND DEFAMATION

Privilege and Defamation

In some instances, something called "privilege" allows a person to make a defamatory statement without fear of prosecution. Absolute privilege exists mainly to be used by courts and legislative bodies. These bodies of government depend on the free exchange of information in order to function properly. Absolute privilege applies to court proceedings, legislative proceedings, some statements and publications from the executive branch, and publications that are required by law. Communications between spouses are also covered by absolute privilege.

Conditional privileges are intended to protect the press from prosecution. In order to claim conditional privilege as a defense, the accused has to prove that he or she believed the statement to be true and had reasonable grounds for believing it to be true. Conditional privileges also include speaking to protect one's own interests, speaking for the benefit of another person, and speaking to report matters of public interest.

Exaggeration and Expression

A lot of writers exaggerate to get their point across. Someone might write that a car is as big as a battleship or that an athlete runs with lightning speed. Obviously, neither statement is literally true, but they get across the point that the car is really big and that the athlete is very fast.

Exaggerating for effect is protected because, while such statements could easily be proven to be false, they are so extreme that no reader would believe them to be literally true. A post accusing an actor of being a space alien would be protected because it is too ridiculous for most reasonable people to take seriously.

Chapter 2

Sifting the Data

Figuring out what makes a source trustworthy or honest can be hard. Most media companies have a professional interest in getting facts right. If they get things wrong on a regular basis, they lose their audience and their advertisers. No one wants to get their news from a source that is inaccurate, and advertisers do not want to be associated with such organizations.

While a lot of information found on the Internet is valuable, there is also a lot of online data that is worthless. The information may be old, inaccurate, or intentionally misleading. This doesn't just apply to online sources. Using old newspapers, magazines, and even books for sources can make your online post out of date and inaccurate. This can be particularly true if you're writing about current events in which the story continues to unfold on a day-to-day basis. In this case, older publications are useful for providing historical context and background to what is happening right now. The Web sites for reputable newspapers, news magazines, and online news organizations should be relied upon to provide up-to-the-minute information on a subject.

In school assignments and reports, teachers want to see accurate information presented clearly. They may ask to see a list of sources that you used

Newspapers and magazines usually have specific sections where letters from readers or essays and opinion pieces from commentators are printed. It is often harder to figure out which Web sites offer slanted opinions rather than objective reporting of fact.

so that they can make sure that the information was presented accurately and came from a reliable source.

Fact or Opinion?

The Internet does not require footnotes, endnotes, or a bibliography for the posts that people put on their personal Web sites, social networking sites, and message boards. Since many people have usernames that they use online in place of their real names, it is often impossible to know exactly who is behind comments posted on the Web. The promise of anonymity can encourage some people to lash out against others. They may hold a grudge against someone they know, such as a former friend or a classmate they resent. Attacks against individuals often consist of insults or rumors.

How can you tell whether or not an online post is factual? There is no sure way, though you can check to see if it is published on a reputable site. Also check to see if it is consistent with other posts.

Some people go online to post attacks against businesses or companies that they feel have slighted them in some way. They may go on message boards or review sites and post rumors in an effort to hurt the business by driving away other customers. There is nothing wrong with writing a negative review or expressing an opinion online. In fact, some businesses appreciate

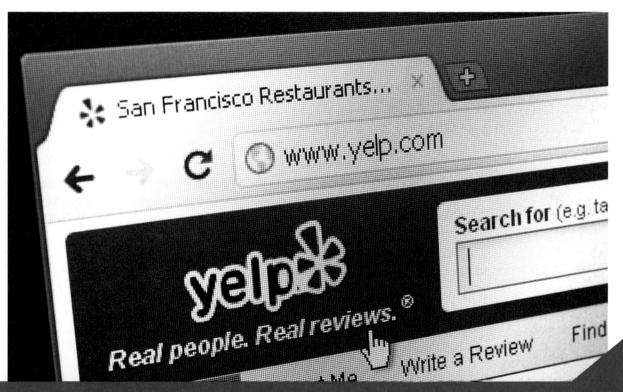

Online review sites such as Yelp.com provide ratings systems to help users decide whether or not they want to visit a business or use a service. These reviews can be skewed by unhappy customers determined to ruin a business's reputation.

legitimate and truthful reviews, even if negative, because it helps them to understand and correct their shortcomings. However, posting information that is not based in fact can be considered defamation. Businesses that have been hit with malicious attacks may lose customers. Their reputations may suffer if they cannot undo the damage caused by the groundless and unsubstantiated online rumors.

Remember that reviews reflect only the opinion of the writer. They may describe his or her experience, but the reviewer's experience may not be the same as that of other customers or consumers. If you're looking at a site that posts ratings and reviews that are submitted by its users, check for common elements in earlier posts. Do users have similar complaints or offer compliments on the same elements, such as decor or the helpfulness of staff members? Finding one or two extremely negative posts amid a range of positive or

---

File   Edit   View   Favorites   Tools   Help

ONLINE REPUTATION MANAGEMENT

Online Reputation Management

In recent years, a growing number of Web sites have started allowing users to post feedback and ratings for businesses and for people who sell items online. These businesses and individuals may lose customers if negative reviews—whether honest or defamatory—come up in search engine results.

Online reputation management is a practice in which negative reviews are pushed to the bottom of search results so that more positive reviews are among those first seen. Reputation management is a growing field for tech companies. Businesses that lack the resources or expertise to constantly monitor what is being said about them online can hire firms such as Reputation.com or Reputation Changer to do it for them. In June 2011, Google even announced that it was making reputation management tools available for free.

even mediocre reviews could be a sign that the reviewer has a personal bias or had an extreme reaction. The same can also be true for rave reviews following a string of less than stellar reviews.

Opinion posts can be found all over the Internet. They may be posted to blogs or message boards. Some are well-reasoned and articulate. They may offer supporting facts and give a fresh perspective on a topic. Others may offer little or no supporting information, ignore facts, and intentionally mislead the reader.

Unless you are analyzing an opinion piece, such as a newspaper column or a review, it is usually best to stay away from using such writings as direct sources. However, they can be useful by pointing you to other sources. While you might not want to use an opinion piece as factual support in your writing, you might be able to track down the source or sources that the opinion piece is based on or reacting to. You can then use that original source and its factual data in your post.

Citing Sources

When posting information from other sources, it is a good idea to name the sources. Naming sources lets readers know where the information in your post comes from and that it wasn't invented or pulled out of thin air by you. Readers can look at the source material and work out how you drew your conclusions. They may agree with what you wrote, or they may have a different perspective on the information presented in your post. People who disagree can use the same information to argue their own viewpoints and broaden the general discussion.

There are many ways to cite sources in an online post. A citation can be worked into a post in such a way that it flows with the text. For example, if you're getting information about a basketball game from a television news show, you can mention the broadcast as your source ("According to ESPN SportsCenter, Kobe Bryant suffered an injury in the second quarter and did not return to the game"). If you don't want to clutter your post with references

« Previous Section   Next Section »

Article Citation:

"Bullying and Cyberbullying." *Teen Health and Wellness*. Rosen Publishing Group, Inc., 2012. Web. 30 May. 2012
<http://www.teenhealthandwellness.com/article/76/bullying-and-cyberbullying>

Footnotes and endnotes are a good way to show your sources without cluttering your writing. These citations usually include the author's name, the title of the work cited, and publication information.

to sources and publications, footnotes or bibliographical notes at the end of your post might be a good alternative to in-text citations.

The Internet also makes it possible to embed hyperlinks to other Web sites within a post. By clicking on the link, readers can go straight to the source that is being referenced. The danger with using embedded hyperlinks is that the links may expire, so when readers click on them they get an error message. You must also be sure to type in the exact Web site or your readers may click to the wrong page or receive an error message. A broken link to another Web site won't be the end of the world for your post, but it can be embarrassing. If the post is part of a school assignment, it could hurt your grade.

Writing for an Audience

Information posted online is intended to be read, or else it would not appear in such a public forum as the Internet. If you are posting online, you may have a good idea of whom you want to find your posts. You might post only on forums that focus on a particular topic or interest, or you might restrict your online presence to keeping a blog and commenting on other blogs.

Your audience may be fairly small and consist mostly of a few friends or family members, or you might have a large number of readers. If you're part of an online community, you may be friends with dozens of people you've never met who read your posts and comment on them.

It is important to understand who your readers are and the sort of posts they expect from you. You may have developed an online persona that is different from how you ordinarily speak and act. You might even have several different identities and personas that you use on different Web sites. The Internet makes it possible to craft a serious persona in one place and a clownish one on another site.

Think about what posts your friends, classmates, and family members might be likely to read. It is easy to write casually about people you know while you're online, but those people might end up reading what you wrote. You may want to avoid writing anything that could hurt their feelings or offend them, even if you are writing under a username. People who are close to you may easily be able to figure out that a username belongs to

Finding an online voice can boost a writer's confidence. Think about what amuses and delights readers without crossing over the line into material that can be hurtful. Family members can provide an ideal "focus group" or test audience.

you. Negative posts can lead to problems once you go offline. Hurt or offended acquaintances may confront you and ask for an apology or an explanation. You may get into trouble with your family or even damage some friendships by being overly critical or careless in how you express yourself.

Also consider the type of information that you would want to see on a Web site. Do you like informative posts covering serious topics, humorous posts, or a mix of both? Do you prefer an edgy voice or one that is more measured? Consider these questions when thinking about the tone of your posts. If most of your posts are on a personal Web site or blog, think about what other design elements you want to include. Do you want photographs or other illustrations? Will you include links to other sites or blogs?

Following the Rules

Keep in mind any rules that your school may have for online posts and Web sites. Some schools have policies that try to regulate what students can post online, though such rules often meet with mixed success. Many schools have found that while they can block social media sites from school computers, students still have access to such sites via smartphones. Efforts to craft policies regarding online posting that extend beyond school hours and school grounds have met with opposition on the grounds that they violate free speech.

Because online posts can be taken down as quickly as they can appear, it can be hard for schools to prove that defamatory comments have been made online. One way in which schools can take action against students who defame others online is if their targets make printouts or save screen shots of the online posts. While the post itself may disappear, the evidence that it existed will remain.

If a post is part of a class assignment, be sure that you understand what sort of information the assignment requires. Teachers will want to see factual and accurate information. They may require you to list sources for your material. The assignment may also call for a more serious or scholarly tone than you normally use online.

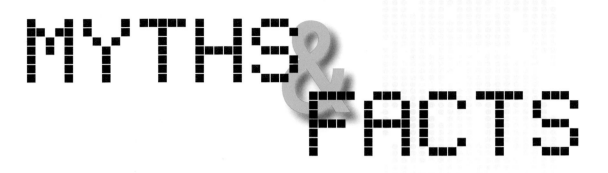

MYTHS & FACTS

MYTH
FACT

Internet posts disappear as soon as they are deleted.
Posts may have already been copied and spread before they were deleted.

MYTH

FACT

Defamation suits can't be brought against a person who posts anonymously.
It may be difficult to pin down who is making anonymous posts, but a case can be made against a specific person if links can be found connecting him or her to the posts.

MYTH

FACT

Any negative statement made against a person can be grounds for a defamation suit.
The law protects free speech by allowing negative statements that are true, are opinion, or are privileged.

Chapter 3

Being Fair

Defamation is not an issue unless you're writing about a specific person or group. It is perfectly acceptable to be critical of people and organizations in online posts. It is even all right to be harsh in your criticism, as long as the criticism can be justified by facts and a sound and reasoned argument. Critical remarks are accepted elements of free speech. The tricky part of expressing your opinion is presenting your criticism in a balanced way that does not defame the subject of your writing.

Using Sources to Protect Yourself

Even if you are careful about the sources that you use, you may still end up posting incorrect information. The best sources sometimes get facts wrong. If you cite the source of the information that you post, however, you can at least show your readers that you made an effort to get factual information.

Citing sources can be particularly important if you are accused of defamation. If you accuse someone of breaking the law, for example, it helps if you can back up your statement with facts gathered from a police report or court documents. If your accusation is based on reports from

Be sure to cite material, even if it comes from a trusted source. Even respected news organizations such as CNN (http://www.cnn.com) occasionally make mistakes in stories.

secondary sources, such as news stories, be sure to cite where you got your information.

It is much harder to defend against accusations of defamation if you base all of your writing on the gossip or personal attacks found in only one source. Try to keep a balanced tone in your posts. Making an attempt to provide both sides of the story that you're trying to tell will show that you're not biased toward one side in particular.

File   Edit   View   Favorites   Tools   Help

ANONYMOUS POSTS

Anonymous Posts

Anonymous posts are one of the biggest stumbling blocks for anyone who has been defamed online. Anonymous posts don't require the writer to identify him- or herself. It is nearly impossible to pin down the identity of someone who is writing anonymous posts.

In the past, anonymous posts have been considered protected speech. There have been several high profile court cases in which people have sued Internet service providers in an attempt to force them to identify the authors of anonymous posts. Most of these attempts failed until April 2012, when a Texas couple managed to successfully sue anonymous Web users who had posted false claims against them on the Topix forum site. A jury awarded the couple $13 million in damages to be paid by six defendants.

Showing Respect

Remember to be respectful. Showing respect for people you don't like and ideas you disagree with will make your comments seem more thoughtful and reasonable. Even people who disagree with you may respect you for the way you write your posts.

Try to avoid using hostile language. You don't have to say things you don't believe, but hostile language can make you appear unreasonable. Some readers may enjoy reading hostile statements and might consider them funny, but others might find them offensive. Hostile language that targets a particular person or group might be read as a threat and could get the writer into trouble. Many schools now have antibullying policies that cover online threats or statements that appear to be threats.

Writing down thoughts and feelings on paper can help you sort out what you want to say online. A post written in the heat of the moment may have lasting and extremely negative consequences.

You might also want to avoid writing posts when you're angry. Think about how a really angry post might sound and how it might make you look after you've calmed down. Writing out your feelings on a piece of paper might help you collect your thoughts and put together a more rational post that expresses your feelings in a more thoughtful way.

Mockery and Satire

Mockery and teasing are common online. A lot of reputable Web sites and writers mock situations, news events, public figures, movies, music, and even

Jon Stewart of Comedy Central's *The Daily Show* satirizes public figures, current events, and television news programs by presenting serious topics in a humorous light.

consumer products online. Some of this mockery is gentle, some of it is savage, and a lot of it falls in between.

Forms of mockery such as satire are protected as free speech. A well-written satire about your school or town could convey your feelings as well as or even better than a straightforward post. However, it is important to take the feelings of the people you are satirizing into account. Will they understand that your satire is good-natured, or will they be hurt or offended by how you portray them?

Take care to think about what you're writing and how it might be interpreted. A line that you intend to be funny may actually offend some people or hurt their feelings. Be sure to read over what you've written before you actually post it to make sure that the meaning of your words is unlikely to be misunderstood. Many satire Web sites include a note stating that the content is meant to be humorous and should not be taken seriously.

Quoting from an opinion piece, like this one posted on Google's Blogger site (http://www .blogger.com), can be a good way to start a dialogue with other people online. Users can post information that supports the opinion or facts that refute it.

Arguing Right and Wrong

If you are using an opinion piece as a source, frame your post as an argument for or against the opinion. Do you agree or disagree with it outright, or do you agree with some parts of it and disagree with others? Explain your thoughts about the opinion and make a case for your reading of the piece. Your readers may be interested in knowing why you feel the way you do, and a well-argued opinion on your part may earn you the respect of people who see your post.

Making a good argument can be tricky. Be sure that you can find reliable information that you can cite in defending your opinion. Keep your argument civil. While opinions are protected from defamation allegations, personal attacks against another writer might not be immune to such charges. You can be witty or sarcastic in your criticism, and you can also word your opinion strongly without attacking the writer on a personal level.

There is a chance that people will respond directly to your post, either by following a thread on a message board or posting notes in a "comments" section. Some people may let you know that they agree with you, while others might tell you why they disagree with your argument. Remember to be civil to both sides. If someone posts a comment that is critical of your writing, you should feel free to respond to him or her. You can post additional evidence that reinforces your argument or information that clarifies your position. You may be tempted to respond rudely if the poster is simply being negative or nasty in his or her comments. Ignore the temptation and instead focus your energy on responding to more responsible posts. You may be able to report the negative poster to the site's managers if his or her writing crosses the line from legitimate criticism to inappropriate, hostile, abusive, or threatening verbal attacks.

TEN GREAT QUESTIONS

TO ASK AN INFORMATION TECHNOLOGY (IT) SPECIALIST

1. Can I get in trouble for accidentally spreading false rumors online?

2. Is it possible to find out who is posting anonymous messages?

3. What makes a post defamatory?

4. What can I do if I am defamed online?

5. Is defamation a form of cyberbullying?

6. How long can an online post remain accessible on the Internet?

7. Can I prove that I have been the target of false rumors if the post has been deleted?

8. Who should I tell if I'm being defamed online?

9. If I post a false rumor, should I apologize?

10. Can a defamed person recover his or her reputation?

Chapter 4

Facing the Consequences

The Internet is constantly changing. Sites may be wildly popular one day and forgotten the next. Whole sites sometimes vanish after their operators pull the plug. Web sites change their content and appearance often in an effort to stay fresh and relevant. Content that was once easy to find may be deleted or sent to archives where it is available only to subscribers or members.

Even though very little stays the same online, Internet posts can be remarkably durable. Every e-mail message ever sent and every word ever posted on a blog is stored on a server somewhere. With a little work, this information could be retrieved. Therefore, what you write and post online may be available forever, able to be read by friends, family members, future romantic partners, in-laws, bosses, coworkers, and even your future children and grandchildren.

The rapid rise of social media outlets makes data more readily available than before. News stories, blog posts, and message board comments are shared among large networks of Internet users. This information is posted, reposted, and sent to a broader audience than might have otherwise seen it.

Wireless technology allows people to access the Internet through mobile devices such as smartphones, broadening the potential audience for Web sites and message boards.

Anyone can now reach a broad online audience. However, how people view you online is based largely on how you treat others in your posts. Do they see you as someone who is unafraid to voice an opinion and does so in a reasoned and intelligent way? Or do they see you as someone who attacks and bullies others online?

Posts Are Forever

Internet posts may be taken down after a few days, but, before that happens, they may be seen by countless people. Others may have copied the posts or quoted from them, so even if the originals were deleted, parts of them could still be circulating online. For most writers, this would be fantastic news. It would mean that their words were being viewed and thought and spoken about by a great many people, and it could bring them more attention.

However, the permanence of online materials can be damaging for someone who writes defamatory statements and posts them online. A post containing lies or misleading information about a person may be deleted soon after it is published, but there is a chance that it has been seen by that person or by people close to him or her. A printout or a screen shot of the post could be used as proof of defamation.

Hurtful online comments might spread quickly, particularly in a close-knit community. For example, a negative post about a classmate or a teacher could be seen by a large number of fellow students in a short period of time

A comment, post, or image intended to be seen by only a few people may reach a much wider audience as friends and family members share it with each other and forward it on to an ever-growing web of digital users.

as people share the comments with each other. Whether they agree or disagree with what is written, the defamatory comments likely will be talked about by a large number of people, and attention will be drawn to the target of the posts and the writer, if he or she is identified.

Writing something damaging about a person and posting it online could continue to hurt the person for years, even if it is removed quickly. Rumors can be very difficult to put to rest, and sometimes a single rumor can lead to more rumors being spread. There have been cases in which people have been forced to leave their school or their job in order to escape untrue rumors. Sometimes the defamatory comments do so much damage to the target's reputation that he or she has to move away. There have even been several high-profile cases in which teens have committed suicide after becoming the victim of online rumor-mongering and bullying, and their tormentors have faced charges in connection with the deaths.

Legal Consequences

Posting defamatory comments can have serious legal consequences for the writer. In order to legally prove defamation took place, the target has to show that the statement was published and that it is false and not an opinion or fact. The target has to be able to show that the post did lasting harm to his or her reputation. It also has to be proven that the writer of the post intended to do harm to the target.

In the United States, defamation cases are usually heard in civil court, meaning that a victory for the accuser would likely result in a monetary award for damages and a public retraction of the damaging statement. There is no federal defamation law, which leaves it up to the states to decide how defamation is prosecuted. The definition of defamation differs from state to state, though the laws of most states include a category of statements called "libel per se." In court, the targets of these libelous statements are not required to prove that they are false. Such libelous statements include claims that the person committed a crime, has a disease, is unfit to carry out his or her business or trade, or has engaged in sexual misconduct.

File   Edit   View   Favorites   Tools   Help

PROTECTED HOSTS

Protected Hosts

Federal law protects Web hosts from being sued for content written by a third party that is posted on their sites. A company like Google is usually immune from defamation suits because it has no control over user content. This means that if a blogger writes a defaming post about someone and makes it public, he or she can be sued, but the company that provides the Web hosting service is protected. The Communication Decency Act of 1996 granted these protections and also placed restrictions on what can be posted online. Most of these restrictions were later struck down as unconstitutional.

Seventeen states and two U.S. territories have criminal defamation laws. The legal penalties for those convicted of criminal defamation can include fines, community service, writing a letter of apology, and even jail time.

Cyberbullying

Writing harassing or untrue posts can also be considered cyberbullying. Cyberbullying is the use of cell phones, computers, chat rooms, e-mails, and messages posted on Web sites to harass or threaten others. Cyberbullies can reach a wide audience while remaining anonymous. A recent study by the Pew Research Center found that about 32 percent of teens said that they had been the target of online harassment, including having rumors spread about them online.

Schools have responded to the growing cyberbullying problem by introducing rules against the practice. Many schools have antibullying

Untrue rumors or other negative comments posted online about fellow students enable bullies to reach out and hurt their targets even when they are away from school.

policies, and in many cases those policies have been updated to include online activity. Most states have also passed laws against cyberbullying, though these laws vary greatly from each other.

Cyberbullies can find themselves accused of defamation. In May 2012, two girls from Cobb County, Georgia, were sued for libel after they created a fake Facebook page for their fourteen-year-old classmate. The fake page included offensive and hurtful false statements about her. The page was eventually taken down after the girl's parents complained about it to Facebook. The two girls responsible were suspended from school for using

Students in Vermont listen to a presentation given by the father of a teenager who killed himself after being bullied online. Schools around the country are working to discourage cyberbullying.

their cell phones to take pictures that were then posted to the fake Facebook page. The incident highlighted the school's lack of a policy against cyber-bullying, as well as the fact that Georgia does not have a law against cyberbullying. It also showed how easy it can be to use social media tools to defame—not to mention impersonate—others.

Laws are still catching up with the speed and ease of communicating online. Steps have been taken in many states to make it harder to defame people online. These steps must be considered with freedom of speech in mind. Lawmakers and schools have to think about the best ways to protect people while preserving a fundamental American right.

GLOSSARY

anonymous Not named or identified.

articulate Expressing oneself freely, clearly, and effectively.

bias An inclination of temperament or outlook, particularly for or against something.

citation An act of quoting.

cyberbullying The electronic posting of mean-spirited and/or threatening messages about a person, often written anonymously.

cyberstalking The use of the Internet to follow, watch, and harass someone in a threatening way.

defamation The act of writing or saying false things in an effort to make people have a bad opinion regarding someone or something.

endnote An explanatory note or citation placed at the end of a chapter, article, or book.

footnote An explanatory note or citation placed at the bottom of the page on which the relevant body text appears.

harassment The act of creating an unpleasant or hostile situation for someone.

libel The illegal act of writing negative and damaging things about a person that are untrue.

mediocre Average or below average in quality, ability, or achievement.

mockery Insulting or contemptuous action or speech.

rumor Unofficial, unsubstantiated information that may or may not be true.

satire The use of humor to criticize someone or something and make them seem silly.

scholarly Having the characteristics of a scholar; academic in content and tone.

slander To make a false spoken statement that leads others to have a bad opinion of someone.

troll Someone who deliberately sends rude or annoying messages to a discussion group on the Internet.

FOR MORE INFORMATION

American Civil Liberties Union (ACLU)
125 Broad Street, 18th Floor
New York NY 10004
(212) 549-2500
Web site: http://www.aclu.org
The American Civil Liberties Union is a nonpartisan organization dedicated
to preserving individual rights as guaranteed by the U.S. Constitution.

American Library Association (ALA)
50 East Huron Street
Chicago, IL 60611
(800) 545-2433
Web site: http://www.ala.org
The American Library Association advocates for access to information and
First Amendment rights.

Canadian Museum for Human Rights
400-269 Main Street
Winnipeg, MB R3C 1B3
Canada
(877) 877-6037
Web site: http://humanrightsmuseum.ca
The Canadian Museum for Human Rights is a place where people can engage
in discussion and commit to taking action against hate and oppression.

Electronic Frontier Foundation
454 Shotwell Street
San Francisco, CA 94110
(415) 436-9333

Web site: https://www.eff.org
The Electronic Frontier Foundation supports free speech on the Internet.

MediaSmarts
950 Gladstone Avenue, Suite 120
Ottawa, ON K1Y 3E6
Canada
(613) 224-7721
Web site: http://mediasmarts.ca
The Media Awareness Network promotes critical thinking about the media.

The Newseum
555 Pennsylvania Avenue NW
Washington, DC 20001
(888) 639-7386
Web site: http://www.newseum.org
The Newseum celebrates the First Amendment to the United States
        Constitution, with a focus on free speech and freedom of the press.

Web Sites

Due to the changing nature of Internet links, Rosen Publishing has developed
an online list of Web sites related to the subject of this book. This site is
updated regularly. Please use this link to access the list:

http://www.rosenlinks.com/DIL/Expr

FOR FURTHER READING

Bingham, Jane. *Internet Freedom: Where Is the Limit?* Chicago, IL: Heinemann-Raintree, 2007.

Brockman, John, ed. *Is the Internet Changing the Way You Think? The Net's Impact on Our Minds and Future*. New York, NY: Harper Perennial, 2011.

Burgan, Michael. *Cornerstones of Freedom: The U.S. Constitution*. Danbury, CT: Children's Press, 2011.

Carr, Nicholas. *The Big Switch: Rewiring the World, from Edison to Google*. New York, NY: W. W. Norton & Co., 2009.

Conway, John. *A Look at the First Amendment: Freedom of Speech and Religion*. Berkeley Heights, NJ: Enslow Publishers, 2008.

Fradin, Dennis. *The Bill of Rights*. Salt Lake City, UT: Benchmark Books, 2008.

Ganchy, Sally, and Claudia Isler. *Understanding Your Right to Free Speech*. New York, NY: Rosen Publishing Group, 2011.

Gerber, Larry. *Cited! Identifying Credible Information Online*. New York, NY: Rosen Publishing Group, 2011.

Haynes, Charles C., et al. *First Freedoms: A Documentary History of First Amendment Rights in America*. New York, NY: Oxford University Press, 2006.

Hunter, Nick. *Internet Safety*. Chicago, IL: Heinemann-Raintree, 2011.

Jones, Molly. *The First Amendment: Freedom of Speech, the Press, and Religion*. New York, NY: Rosen Publishing Group, 2011.

Leavitt, Aime. *The Bill of Rights*. Newark, DE: Mitchell Lane Publishers, 2011.

MacEachern, Robyn. *Cyberbullying: Deal with It and Ctl Alt Delete It*. Toronto, ON: Lorimer Publishing, 2009.

Marcovitz, Hal. *Online Information and Research*. San Diego, CA: ReferencePoint Press, 2011.

Merino, Noel. *Censorship*. Detroit, MI: Greenhaven Press, 2010.

Parks, Peggy. *Online Social Networking*. San Diego, CA: ReferencePoint Press, 2011.

Pascaretti, Vicki. *Super Smart Information Strategies: Team Up Online*. Ann Arbor, MI: Cherry Lake Publishing, 2010.

Smith, Richard E. *The First Amendment: The Right of Expression*. Minneapolis, MN: ABDO and Daughters, 2007.

Yahoo! *The Yahoo! Style Guide: The Ultimate Sourcebook for Writing, Editing, and Creating Content for the Digital World*. New York, NY: St. Martin's Griffin, 2010.

BIBLIOGRAPHY

Alaimo, Jessica. "Schools Look for Solutions to Challenges of New Technology." *Chillicothe Gazette*, May 7, 2012. Retrieved May 2012 (http://www.chillicothegazette.com/article/20120507/NEWS01/205070304).

Associated Press. "Court Asked If Schools Can Punish MySpace Parodies." *Legal Intelligencer*, June 3, 2010. Retrieved May 2012 (http://www.law.com/jsp/pa/PubArticlePA.jsp?id=1202459145995&slreturn=1).

Associated Press. "Judge: Media Must Reveal IDs of Online Posters." *Anderson Herald Bulletin*, March 6, 2011. Retrieved May 2012 (http://heraldbulletin.com/crime/x831629250/Judge-Media-must-reveal-IDs-of-online-posters).

Associated Press. "State Appeals Court Overturns Anonymous Commenter Ruling." *Merrillville Post-Tribune*, February 21, 2012. Retrieved May 2012 (http://posttrib.suntimes.com/news/10790252-418/state-appeals-court-overturns-anonymous-commenter-ruling.html).

Campbell, Elizabeth. "Joking Between Friends Becomes Texas Supreme Court Case." *Fort Worth Star-Telegram*, March 19, 2012. Retrieved May 2012 (http://www.star-telegram.com/2012/03/18/3818710/joking-between-friends-becomes.html).

Charisse, Marc. "Nothing to Like About Facebook Libel Suit." *Evening Sun*, May 5, 2012. Retrieved May 2012 (http://www.eveningsun.com/edcolumn/ci_20539674/nothing-like-about-facebook-libel-suit).

Clark, Doug. "Libel Happens Online, Too." *Greensboro News-Record*, May 1, 2012. Retrieved May 2012 (http://www.news-record.com/blog/54431/entry/142818).

Fairfax News. "Florida Plastic Surgeon Hopes to Unmask Online Critic in Virginia Courts." May 4, 2012. Retrieved May 2012 (http://fairfaxnews.com/2012/05/florida-plastic-surgeon-hopes-to-unmask-online-critic-in-virginia-courts).

Gorner, Jeremy, and Jason Meisner. "For Victims of Unfounded Online Attacks, Clearing Your Name Can Be Frustrating." *Chicago Tribune*, April 26, 2012. Retrieved May 2012 (http://articles.chicagotribune.com/2012-04-26/news/ct-met-online-sidebar-20120426_1_yelp-websites-and-internet-service-review-site).

Heussner, Ki Mae, and Susanna Kim. "Jury Awards $13 Million in Texas Defamation Suit Against 'Anonymous' Posters." ABC News, April 24, 2012. Retrieved May 2012 (http://abcnews.go.com/Business/jury-awards-13-million-texas-defamation-suit-anonymous/story?id=16194071).

Lenhart, Amanda. "One in Three Online Teens Have Experienced Online Harassment." Pew Research Center, June 27, 2007. Retrieved May 2012 (http://www.pewinternet.org/Reports/2007/Cyberbullying/1-Findings.aspx).

Lewis, Anthony. *Freedom for the Thought That We Hate: A Biography of the First Amendment*. New York, NY: Basic Books, 2008.

Nusca, Andrew. "Defamation or Free Speech? US Court Orders Google to Hand Over Identity of Blogger." ZDNet, August 20, 2009. Retrieved May 2012 (http://www.zdnet.com/blog/btl/defamation-or-free-speech-us-court-orders-google-to-hand-over-identity-of-blogger/23009).

Packard, Ashley. *Digital Media Law*. Malden, MA: John Wiley and Sons, 2010.

Perez, Juan Carlos. "Google Tackles Online Reputation Management." *PC World*, July 15, 2011. Retrieved May 2012 (http://www.pcworld.com/article/230362/google_tackles_online_reputation_management.html).

Tedford, Thomas, and Dale Herbeck. *Freedom of Speech in the United States*. State College, PA: Strata Publishing Company, 2009.

Turner, Dorie, and Greg Bluestein. "Cyberbullying Victims Fight Back in Lawsuits." *Charleston Gazette*, April 28, 2012. Retrieved May 2012 (http://charleston-gazette.vlex.com/vid/cyberbullying-victims-fight-lawsuits-369826398).

INDEX

About the Author

Jason Porterfield is a writer and journalist who has written extensively about politics, law, constitutional law, current events, digital technology, social networking, and culture. His information technology-related titles include *Conducting Basic and Advanced Searches* and *Careers as a Cyberterrorism Expert*. Porterfield lives in Chicago, Illinois.

Photo Credits

Cover and p. 1 (left) © iStockphoto.com/CGinspiration; cover and p. 1 (middle left), p. 8 Brendan O'Sullivan/Photolibrary/Getty Images; cover and p. 1 (middle right), p. 37 Ron Levine/The Image Bank/Getty Images; cover and p. 1 (right), pp. 17, 25 © iStockphoto.com/Günay Mutlu; p. 5 Ingram Publishing/Thinkstock; pp. 12, 34 Monkey Business Images/Shutterstock.com; p. 16 Purestock/Getty Images; p. 21 Todd Warnock/Lifesize/Thinkstock; p. 27 Monkey Business/Thinkstock; pp. 28, 38 © AP Images; p. 29 © David Young-Wolff/PhotoEdit; p. 33 Vicky Kasala Productions/Photodisc/Getty Images; cover (background) and interior page graphics © iStockphoto.com/suprun.

Designer: Nicole Russo; Photo Researcher: Karen Huang